# The Path
## to
# Forgiveness

# Dedication

To my mother, who modeled and taught me
about forgiveness through the many times she
told me to "forget about it," and also to those
who have given me the gift of forgiveness.

Scripture quotations on pages 13, 53, and 88 are from THE HOLY BIBLE, NEW INTERNATIONAL
VERSION®, NIV® Copyright © 1973, 1978, 1984, 2011 by Biblica, Inc.® Used by persmission. All rights
reserved worldwide.

Library of Congress Cataloging-in-Publication data is available upon request.
ISBN: 978-1-68088-216-2

**M** and Blue Mountain Press are registered in U.S. Patent and Trademark Office.
Certain trademarks are used under license.

Printed in China.
First Printing: 2018

This book is printed on recycled paper.

This book is printed on paper that has been specially produced to be acid free (neutral pH) and contains no
groundwood or unbleached pulp. It conforms with the requirements of the American National Standards
Institute, Inc., so as to ensure that this book will last and be enjoyed by future generations.

## Blue Mountain Arts, Inc.
P.O. Box 4549, Boulder, Colorado 80306

# The Path
## to
# Forgiveness

*Moving forward with
hope and healing
one day at a time*

Dr. Preston C. VanLoon

**Blue Mountain Press**™
Boulder, Colorado

# TABLE OF CONTENTS

# INTRODUCTION

Perhaps you or someone you know is suffering from undeserved hurt and pain. Or maybe you are attempting to recover from a past wrong and need a new beginning in life or a relationship. *The Path to Forgiveness* is for those who want, and need, to heal from being unjustly offended by another.

Forgiveness is a mindset and way of living that is worth the effort and benefits it offers. Healing doesn't happen overnight or just by saying the words "I forgive you." The decision to forgive involves a willingness to acknowledge and respond in a positive manner to the wrong that has been done to you.

Once you choose to forgive and start practicing forgiveness strategies, you will begin to experience the advantages of forgiveness. Keep in mind, though, that forgiveness is a gradual process and that healing and hope develop one day at a time.

The intent of this book is to help guide you from the suffering you are feeling to renewed peace of mind and meaning in your life. Each meditation includes a "For Reflection" question for further contemplation as it applies to your own situation. Following each question is an "Affirmation," or positive thought to embrace, that supports and relates to the content of the meditation.

If you are further along in the forgiveness process, but are having difficulty in some area, you may find it helpful to go back to a specific meditation to address the particular issue you may need to work on. The quotes, meditations, reflections, and affirmations are all designed to keep you actively engaged in the forgiveness and healing process.

Forgiveness requires being able to transform and use your energy effectively to help you move forward in life. As you begin to heal, you will be rewarded by favorable changes in your thoughts, feelings, and behaviors, and you will experience the desired outcomes and benefits of forgiveness.

Welcome to the path to forgiveness.

Preston C. VanLoon

# Acknowledging the Hurt and Pain

Forgiveness begins with acknowledging that you have been unjustly hurt by another. You might think about how the offense has adversely changed your life, perhaps permanently, and how your thoughts, feelings, and behaviors have been affected by your injury.

You may have a negative perception of the person who hurt you and think your life is worse now compared to theirs. Thoughts of revenge or retaliation may persist. You might even question whether there is justice and fairness in the world.

It's also possible that intense feelings of anger, bitterness, resentment, shame, and hatred have taken over your life. Behavioral and physical symptoms may be present too. You may avoid going to certain places or being around specific people. Changes in your sleeping patterns and appetite might even be noticed.

Developing an awareness of these thoughts, feelings, and behaviors provides the foundation for forgiveness and healing in your life.

# 1
# The Weight of the Offense

*The rain falls because the clouds can no longer handle the weight. The tears fall because the heart can no longer handle the pain.*

— *Author Unknown*

Being mistreated by someone can weigh heavily on you and cause a lot of anxiety and mental stress in your life, work, and relationships. Sometimes the weight of what occurred can even seem too great to endure.

Consider this story: A professor was giving a lecture to a group of students on stress management. As he walked around the room, he raised a glass of water and asked his class how much it weighed. Many of the students suggested the glass weighed various amounts depending on how much water was in it. The professor then explained to the class that the weight of the glass didn't matter. He said that what matters is how long he held the glass. The longer he held on to it, the heavier it became.

The same is true when you suffer from an undeserved offense. The longer you hold on to what happened, the heavier it becomes for you and the more difficult it is to manage your life and relationships. You may even be so accustomed to living with the troublesome pain of the wrong that was done to you that it has become part of your life. You find it difficult to let go, so you continue to tolerate the agony.

Such was the case for a sixty-year-old woman who was admitted to a psychiatric unit of a hospital after her father died. For many years, she had been holding on to the pain of something her father had done to her as a young girl. Over time, the terrible offense became heavier and heavier and began to affect her relationships and ability to enjoy life. When she chose to forgive, it felt like a tremendous weight was finally lifted off her shoulders, and she was free to move on with her life.

The sooner you commit to forgiveness and work through the difficult feelings and thoughts you are experiencing, the less impact the weight of the offense will have on you. Then you will finally feel a sense of freedom and relief with a renewed lease on life.

For Reflection: How has the stress of not being able to let go of your hurt caused difficulty in your life?

Affirmation: I choose to let go of the suffering I have been carrying around in my life so I can be free and move forward with healing and hope.

# 2
# The Emotional Struggle

*Forgiveness is better than revenge.*
*The one shows native gentleness,*
*the other savagery.*

— *Epictetus*

When you have been severely and unfairly hurt, it can have an overwhelming effect on your life. John was abused when he was a young boy by someone he liked and trusted. As he grew into his early teens and twenties, he could not stop thinking about what had happened to him. He became confused and felt shame and guilt, and his self-esteem gradually decreased.

John struggled with a mixture of emotions, including depression, anxiety, and anger. He even considered suicide at times. He began acting out, avoided certain people, and his school grades declined. John suffered from post-traumatic stress symptoms; he was diagnosed with depression and eventually hospitalized. Later in life, he learned about forgiveness and gradually found strength through his faith and counseling to let go of his past hurt.

Maybe you have been poorly treated or suffered traumatic events in your life and can relate to some of the same thoughts, feelings, and behaviors described in John's story. You are not alone in your pain.

You may feel embarrassment and shame, be afraid to tell others about what occurred, and struggle with low self-esteem. You may find it difficult to stop thinking about the terrible wrongs you were subjected to. You may even have difficulties sleeping and problems with your appetite.

Like John, when you make the decision to consider forgiveness as a choice for your life, your healing journey begins. The path to forgiveness frees you from the strong, painful emotions and troubling thoughts that have haunted you.

Instead of being controlled by your negative emotions and dwelling on the mistreatment you endured, forgiveness gives you the strength to let go of past wrongs and continue on with your life. It helps you invest your energy in what is beneficial and will bring peace and healing to your wounds.

Through forgiveness, you will find the courage and strength to focus on your wellness, not the hurt, and your future, not the past. As healing begins, you will experience a sense of freedom from what had brought you pain. You will also be able to focus on what brings meaning and peace of mind to your life and helps you to feel better about yourself.

For Reflection: How does the hurt and pain you suffer from affect your energy and self-esteem?

Affirmation: I will focus on the thoughts and emotions that bring healing and meaning to my life.

# 3
# The Anger

*Fools give full vent to their rage,*
*but the wise bring calm in the end.*

— *Proverbs 29:11 (NIV)*

The anger you feel from being treated awfully can trigger your desire for revenge. You may lie awake at night obsessing and rehearsing in your mind over and over again the hurtful action that was done to you. In your anger, you might think of ways to retaliate. Such thoughts are a normal reaction when you have been mistreated.

People who have been wronged and suffer unfairly often develop negative opinions about those who have injured them. They may think of their offender as being evil or mean-spirited. They may wonder how one human being could treat another in such a hurtful way. In their anger, they may cry out for justice and hope that the person who hurt them suffers equally or more.

A lot of mental and emotional energy can be expended when your life has been adversely affected by an unjustifiable act done by another. Sometimes the anger becomes so intense that you release it in unhealthy and destructive ways by hurting others or yourself even more. This negative energy can be distressing and exhausting.

If you allow feelings of anger, bitterness, and resentment and thoughts of revenge to continue affecting your life, your future could become worse. Upon reflection, you may not like the person you have become.

Though anger in and of itself is not bad and can be a source of motivation for change, it can also be unproductive if you do not handle it in a healthy and positive manner. Anger can challenge you to rise above the hurt you experienced.

Making a better choice for your life begins when you redirect the negative energy you feel and focus on the healing you need. Only light can overcome the darkness in your life. Revenge and judgment are best left up to God. More than anything else, you need to heal.

Forgiveness is a challenging journey that brings healing to feelings of anger and rage, restoring a sense of calm and direction to your life. As you learn to let go of your intense emotions and forgive those who have hurt you, your suffering will diminish and hope for your future will be rekindled.

For Reflection: How might pursuing the path to forgiveness help you more than holding on to your anger?

Affirmation: I will walk the path to forgiveness one day at a time and use my energy for what is helpful and good for my well-being.

# 4
# Feelings of Shame

*The most terrifying thing is to accept oneself completely.*

— Carl Jung

$\mathcal{S}$hame can be one of the most difficult mental states to cope with when you have been hurt. Sometimes the shame and embarrassment you feel from what was done to you can be overwhelming and make you want to disappear from the world. It can cause you to feel worthless, unwanted, and not good enough.

Several years ago, my wife and I had a golden retriever named Champ. On a couple of occasions when we came home after being out, Champ did not greet us at the door as he usually would with a smile on his face and his tail wagging. Instead, with a hint of shame, he slowly walked up to us with his tail tucked between his hind legs and his head down. It would not be long before we found the plastic wrapper from a loaf of bread lying on the floor with the bread nowhere to be seen.

Shame can make it difficult for you to effectively cope with what has occurred. Thoughts of inadequacy and feelings of anxiety and depression may cause you to withdraw and avoid being around certain people. Or you may try to please others to gain their acceptance.

When you have been hurt in a shameful manner, you may sometimes assume fault for what took place. You may think you are responsible and did something wrong to provoke someone. Instead of holding the offender responsible for their actions, you begin to blame yourself for what happened.

Forgiveness adds value to your life and reminds you that your life does matter. It affirms your worth, brings healing to your shame, and restores meaning and direction to who you are. Forgiveness is being fair to yourself; the hurt and painful emotions you suffered are unfair.

Forgiveness also restores your self-confidence. It empowers you to replace the negative thoughts and feelings you are experiencing with those that are healthy and add passion to your life. It helps you realize that what happened to you does not define who you are.

For Reflection: How has shame from the wrong you experienced affected your life?

Affirmation: My self-worth is not based on the shame I feel or the wrong done to me, but on the person I am deep inside and my value in God's eyes.

# 5
# The Inability to Forget

*Genuine forgiveness does not deny
anger but faces it head-on.*

— Alice Duer Miller

I'm sure you have heard the words "forgive and forget." However, there are many who say they are unable to forgive because they cannot forget. When you have been significantly hurt by another and the incident has had an unpleasant effect on your life, forgetting can be difficult, if not impossible. Your injury, whether it is physical or emotional, may leave scars that you will carry with you for the rest of your life.

This was the case for Immaculée Ilibagiza. Her entire family, except for one brother, and approximately 800,000 others were killed in the 1994 massacre that took place in Rwanda when members of the Tutsi ethnic group were slaughtered. During the three-month siege, Ilibagiza hid in a concealed bathroom along with seven other women. When the disturbing atrocity ended, she had lost fifty pounds. Yet after all her suffering, she knew that if she was going to survive, she would need to let go of the anger and hatred that consumed her from all the killing that had taken place around her.

Despite the horrible events of the genocide, Ilibagiza realized that the only thing she had left to give was forgiveness. By letting go of the hatred and thoughts of revenge that consumed her, she eventually came to the point where she could let go and wish the best for those who had hurt her. While others would have shown contempt toward the killers, Ilibagiza chose forgiveness.

Forgiveness does not require that you forget what happened. Rarely, when you have suffered an awful injury, will you ever forget. Instead of dwelling on the offense and the negative emotions that overwhelm you, serenity is found when you choose to release what has hurt you by focusing on what will heal you. This was true for Ilibagiza who, despite her memories, felt peace in her heart when she came face to face with the man who had killed her mother and brother.

Ilibagiza knew that anger, revenge, and hatred toward her offenders would not bring back her family or change the suffering and loss she endured. If she was going to continue on with her life in a meaningful way it was necessary for Ilibagiza to forgive.

For Reflection: Where are you in your life with letting go of the painful memory and powerful, unpleasant emotions that have affected your recovery?

Affirmation: I will experience serenity and be able to continue on in my life when I commit to forgiveness.

# 6
# Thoughts of Revenge

*This is certain, that a man that studieth revenge keeps his own wounds green, which otherwise would heal and do well.*

— Francis Bacon

When you have been horribly mistreated, it is not uncommon to scream out for revenge. You want to make sure the person who hurt you doesn't get away with what they did to you.

There is the story of the farmer who wanted to be certain that the fox who was stealing his chickens would never do it again. So he set a trap and caught the fox. Then he soaked the tail of the fox with gasoline and set it on fire. When the fox realized that his tail was burning, he took off running through the farmer's wheat field, which had not yet been harvested. As a result, the farmer sustained even more loss, losing not only his chickens but his harvest too.

When you take matters into your own hands, your situation often becomes worse and your suffering more complicated. The desire to punish those who caused your hurt and pain lowers you to the same level as them. In your distress and quest for revenge, you become just like the person who offended you.

By choosing to pay back "an eye for an eye," you will not only need to work through the negative emotions and thoughts you have from the initial hurt, but you may also need to deal with the guilt and shame you feel from seeking revenge.

In the long run, you may realize that revenge is not sweet, nor does it help you to improve or feel better. Revenge keeps the wrong you suffered fresh in your mind and prolongs your pain without offering any closure to your wounds or healing to your damaged emotions.

Forgiveness, on the other hand, is a sign of strength. It helps you recover from what happened to you and regain momentum in your life. The best revenge you can pursue is your personal well-being and success. In doing so, you rise above the wrong that was done to you. You prove to yourself, and to those who offended you, that you are a better person and cannot be kept down.

Pursuing revenge will only take you in the opposite direction of where you need to go. It may also inflict more distress on you and others. When you choose to forgive, you are letting go of the desire to hurt those who have mistreated you by choosing a better way for yourself.

For Reflection: How have thoughts of revenge kept you from progressing and retaking control over your life?

Affirmation: Choosing not to pursue revenge and to overcome evil with good will help me heal and experience greater meaning and purpose in my life.

# 7
# The Demand for Justice

*Spare me through your mercy,*
*lest you exact retribution through your justice.*

— Anselm of Canterbury

The demand for justice is strong when someone unfairly injures you. You might attempt to pursue "justice" on your own or consider using the legal system. You may want to make sure the person who hurt you gets what is coming to them and does not get away with what they have done.

Seeking justice should not be confused with the desire for revenge. Justice is often a public event that involves using the legal process to resolve an offense. Revenge is usually more personal, involving the desire to retaliate or get even with the person who hurt you.

Patricia lost her husband when he went for a walk to buy a newspaper and didn't return home. While looking for him, she came upon the scene where he had been struck and killed by a car. Later, choosing not to harbor ill feelings, Patricia wrote a letter to the driver stating that despite how difficult her loss was, it was probably much worse for the driver.

When you have experienced an undeserved offense, you may be conflicted between the pursuit of justice and showing forgiveness. Justice not only involves condemning the hurtful action as wrong but may also include punishing the offender. Its primary aim is to satisfy the need of society and correct the injustice that has been done. In some cases, a wrong may never be made right in your eyes. When you pursue justice, you place your future and trust in the legal system to do what it believes is best.

Forgiveness is something that comes from within and that you have control over. While it identifies the external wrong done to you, the focus is on using your inner energy to pursue healing. Forgiveness acknowledges what occurred but realizes that to continue with hope and meaning in your life, healing needs to happen from within your heart and mind.

When you forgive, you let go of the desire to punish your offender and relegate the quest for justice to God who is the perfect judge. You realize that no amount of justice from an imperfect legal system will help you heal from your hurt. Forgiveness allows you to regain power over your life and focus on the healing you need, so hope may be restored.

For Reflection: How has the desire for justice affected your willingness to consider forgiveness as a possibility to help you heal?

Affirmation: When I let go of the desire to punish my offender and choose to forgive, I begin to heal and regain control over my life and my future.

# 8
# Consumed by Hatred

*Be kind, for everyone you meet
is fighting a hard battle.*

— *John Watson*

Hatred is an intense emotion that can easily lead to destructive and harmful thoughts or actions toward another.

Sadly, this is what happened in 2016 when forty-nine people were killed and over fifty injured inside the Pulse nightclub in Orlando, Florida. The twenty-nine-year-old shooter, who had pledged himself to the terrorist group ISIS, committed one of the worst acts of violence and hate in US history.

Upon hearing that their daughter had been one of the victims, her family immediately drove to Florida where they heard the terrible news of her death. They were overwhelmed with a variety of emotions, including disbelief, anger, and sadness. Yet the father was determined not to let his suffering and loss destroy his life. Instead of responding with the same hatred as the shooter, he saw that the best way to heal from his pain was through forgiveness.

Hatred often says more about the person holding it than the person toward whom it is directed. Hatred is fueled by anger and resentment that builds over time affecting your well-being. Harboring hatred can consume your thinking and cause you to act in a vengeful and inappropriate manner. The longer you delay releasing your distressing feelings, the worse it is for you.

Elaine felt angry, bitter, and full of hate upon learning her sister had been murdered as a result of a man setting fire to her house. She blamed God and felt lonely and lost. When Elaine heard her priest speak about forgiveness, he described hatred as being like a cancer that continues to grow until it destroys you. At that moment, she knew that she had to ask God to forgive her hatred and to give her the strength to forgive the man who killed her sister. When she did, she felt a weight lifted from her.

Dwelling on your undeserved offenses creates a climate for hatred to develop. You become a victim not only of the wrong you suffered but also of your hatred. These negative feelings continue to have power over your life and hinder your ability to have meaningful relationships.

When you forgive, you give up the right to hate the person who unjustly hurt you so you can heal. Peace of mind and goodness are restored to your life when you invest your energy in showing love to those who wronged you.

For Reflection: What effect have hatred and anger from being unjustly hurt had in your life and relationships?

Affirmation: When someone wrongs me, I will respond in a manner that is constructive, not destructive, and that reflects love, not hate.

# 9
# Carrying a Grudge

*I firmly believe a great many
prayers are not answered because we are
not willing to forgive someone.*

— *Dwight L. Moody*

Holding a grudge can be devastating and have life-changing implications.

Jim began looking for another job when he felt unappreciated and slighted at work for his contribution on a team project. He had not been recognized by his superiors, while his colleague had been awarded with a raise.

Sarah felt neglected by her father because he spent more time with her brother than with her and didn't show much interest in her accomplishments. So she began seeking attention from others in unhealthy ways.

Hanging on to grudges can wear you out. As resentment takes root in your heart, it can keep you from receiving much-needed healing and experiencing enjoyment in life. The following story describes this point.

A mother was trying to teach her daughter the benefits of practicing forgiveness and how it would help her feel happier.

So she took the little girl's backpack and filled it with large rocks. The mother asked her daughter to walk around the house wearing the backpack for a few hours while she played with her toys and did her chores. Eventually, the backpack became very heavy and the young girl got tired and told her mother she wanted to rest.

The mother then sat down with her daughter and explained what she was trying to teach her about forgiveness. She told her that each rock in the backpack represented the different feelings of anger, bitterness, hatred, resentment, and revenge that people keep inside them when they hold a grudge.

Then the mother explained to her daughter how the longer you carry those unhealthy emotions and thoughts inside you, the heavier they become and the more tired you feel. Forgiveness, instead, lightens your suffering, freeing up more energy for you to enjoy life.

By forgiving those who have done you wrong, your burdens and grudges are released, offering healing and renewed hope to your life and relationships.

For Reflection: What are some of the grudges and heavy emotions you have been carrying around inside your heart that you need to let go of to make your burden lighter?

Affirmation: I will release the grudges and agony I have been feeling, so I can enjoy better health and relationships with others.

# 10
# Accepting the Wrong

*Every blade has two edges;*
*he who wounds with the one is wounded*
*with the other.*

— *Victor Hugo*

Your initial response to being hurt may be one of denial or disbelief. It may be difficult for you to imagine that your life has been so significantly and adversely affected by the wrong inflicted on you.

Kathy could not believe it when her husband of seven years said he wanted a divorce. They had one child, had been high school sweethearts, and came from the same community. She began blaming herself and wondering what she had done wrong. She even tried doing things differently for him, but nothing changed his mind. This was something she never thought would happen to her.

Accepting the reality of an unexpected wrong you suffered is important for the healing process to begin so you can go on with your life. You cannot change what you do not accept.

Admitting that someone has hurt you does not mean that you are condoning or excusing the injury. It also does not mean ignoring the anger, loss, sadness, and resentment you feel. Acceptance means you have come to the realization that your life has been changed and you are not the same as you were before. You realize that the loss you sustained may never be replaced and may even be gone forever. You know that from now on, your life will be different than it used to be and that there will be a new normal.

You also recognize, as evidenced from others' experiences, that life offers many second and third chances. You gain strength to continue when you cease denying that the injury happened, concede that you were unfairly treated, and commit to the journey of rebuilding your life. The hurt you suffered need not define or change who you are at your core. In fact, it has the potential to make you a better person, if you choose.

The path to forgiveness gives you the opportunity to heal and grow from your painful circumstances. By committing to forgiveness, you accept the hurt that occurred, reflect on and learn from your past, and choose to live with hope and purpose one day at a time.

**For Reflection:** How will accepting the wrong that was done to you help you leave the past behind and find a new direction for your life?

**Affirmation:** When I make the decision to forgive, I will learn from my wounds and not live in them.

# Making the Decision to Forgive

When you suffer from being mistreated, you have a choice. You can choose to hold on to the anger, hatred, resentment, and other painful emotions you feel and allow them to continue to adversely affect the quality of your life, health, and relationships. Or you can make the decision to take control of your healing and commit to the practice of interpersonal forgiveness.

You may not have had a choice about the wrong you experienced, but you can decide whether you will seek a favorable resolution to what happened. Hopefully you will recognize that choosing the path to forgiveness offers the healing you desire, as well as the possibility for a new beginning.

When you make the decision to forgive, you are retaking control over your life and your future. Forgiveness allows you to once again find meaning and direction in life.

# 11
# What Is Forgiveness?

*No act of kindness,
no matter how small,
is ever wasted.*

— Aesop

Forgiveness is often misunderstood. Is it simply saying the words "I forgive you"? Does it mean letting the person who offended you off the hook? Does forgiveness require you to become vulnerable again and open yourself to being hurt and mistreated? Or is forgiveness a matter of letting time heal your wounds? When you hear the word "forgiveness," what thoughts come to your mind?

Let me begin by sharing a few ideas of what forgiveness is not. First, forgiveness does not mean forgetting about the wrong you suffered and going back to living the way things were before. If you have been significantly hurt by someone, rarely will you ever be the same as you were before the hurtful act or will you forget that it ever occurred.

Second, some may suggest that forgiveness should only be given to those who ask for forgiveness and apologize for their behavior. But what if the person who hurt you is not sorry? Perhaps they are unaware of how deeply you were affected. Or you may not even know or have access to this person, especially if they are deceased or no longer in your life.

Forgiveness is not the same as reconciliation. Forgiveness is a courageous decision that comes out of your own interest and impetus. Reconciliation happens externally when two or more people come together again.

When you forgive, you are not condoning, excusing, or pardoning the behavior of your offender. Nor are you just putting up with or making excuses for the unjust offense. The person who hurt you is still responsible and accountable for their actions. Forgiveness is also not a matter of passively ignoring your angry feelings and letting them diminish over time.

Forgiveness is a decision you make to pursue healing from an unfair, harmful incident by letting go of the disturbing thoughts, feelings, and behaviors it has caused. It's choosing to transform burdensome emotional and mental energy from what happened into healthy and constructive actions through the practices of compassion, empathy, and benevolence, regardless of whether the person who hurt you deserves it.

For Reflection: How does making the choice to forgive compare with other possible alternatives you may have considered?

Affirmation: By making the decision to forgive, I can transform the painful, negative energy I am feeling into something that is beneficial and will help me heal.

# 12
# Why Forgive?

*Forgiveness is a virtue*
*of the brave.*

— Indira Gandhi

Forgiving those who hurt you can be very difficult depending on the nature and severity of what occurred. You may not want to forgive because you think of your offender only through the eyes of the wrong you suffered. You may also believe that this person does not deserve forgiveness because of how you were mistreated.

When you do not forgive, your focus tends to be more on your affliction rather than on the healing you need. You become preoccupied with how the offense and feelings of resentment, anger, and bitterness have affected the quality of your life. Neglecting to let go of these emotions can place a burden on your heart and prevent you from moving on with your life and experiencing peace of mind.

Withholding forgiveness binds you to the memories of your past and impedes necessary healing from taking place. It hinders you from reclaiming control of your life. The hurt you suffered may also have a ripple effect, negatively affecting other people you care about.

Holding on to your pain can keep you stuck in a victim mentality. It allows your offender to continue having power over you. Forgiveness is a gift that puts you back in the driver's seat and changes the direction of your future.

Research has found that there are several health benefits that come from forgiving. It suggests that practicing forgiveness decreases depression and anxiety, helps prevent the escalation of revenge, improves personal and interpersonal peace, reduces insomnia, and decreases digestive problems. Another study concluded that there is a positive correlation between the practice of forgiveness and the amount of joy one feels.

When you do not forgive, you allow your suffering to continue and you remain bound to the wrongs of your past. Forgiveness helps you heal holistically with renewed purpose and vision for your life. Forgiving empowers you to let go of your distressing feelings, regain inner strength, and find meaning and energy once again.

For Reflection: How has not forgiving the person who hurt you negatively affected who you are?

Affirmation: Forgiving those who have wronged me will have a positive effect on my future and wellness.

# 13
# Forgiveness Is Difficult

*Hating people is like burning down your own house to get rid of a rat.*

— *Harry Emerson Fosdick*

Choosing to respond to an unwarranted, painful experience with forgiveness is not easy. Some offenses, depending on their severity and nature, may be more difficult to let go of than others.

Perhaps you've heard some people say that they could never forgive someone if they did "such and such." How you respond and whether you forgive can have a significant effect on the future of your life.

There is a story about a young boy who once approached his grandfather and asked his opinion about all the fighting and conflict in the world. The grandfather responded that he felt like two wolves were fighting in his heart. One of them was full of anger and hatred, and the other was full of love, peace, and forgiveness. The boy then asked his grandfather which of the wolves would win. The grandfather responded that the one that will win is the one he feeds.

The same is true when you are hurt. On the one hand, you may feel anger, bitterness, and resentment. On the other, you also know that seeking revenge and retaliation for a wrong you encountered may only make matters worse for you and not help you heal.

One man agonized with such a dilemma when his wife of ten years was raped and murdered. Prior to the charges being read against the individuals who perpetrated the horrible crime, he said that everything in him wanted to hate, be angry, and slip into despair. Instead, he chose the path of forgiveness, grace, and hope. He had learned from the years he spent with his wife that allowing his wounded feelings, rather than what he truly feels and believes in his heart and mind, to drive his decisions was a recipe for hopelessness and a poor outcome.

Your reaction to the hurtful act that was done to you can make all the difference in your future. What you feed with your time, attention, and energy will dominate your life and determine your fate.

It is important not to base your decision to forgive on how you feel, but rather on what will restore a sense of peace and contentment to your well-being.

For Reflection: What are you feeding the hurt and pain in your life?

Affirmation: I am not accountable for the hurtful actions of others, but I am responsible for how I respond to those behaviors and the choices I make for my healing.

# 14
## Forgiveness Is a Process

*A wise man will make haste to forgive, because
he knows the true value of time, and will not suffer
it to pass away in unnecessary pain.*

— *Samuel Johnson*

Forgiveness may be one of the most difficult decisions you will ever make. When you have been significantly mistreated, you might want to fix your heartache too quickly, without taking the time to actively work through the loss and emotional pain you may be feeling.

As you begin to heal from your suffering, it is imperative to remember that forgiveness is a process more than it is a destination. It takes time and effort and doesn't occur overnight.

It is also crucial to keep in mind that loss is part of the hurt you suffered, and your life may suddenly no longer be the same. The loss you experienced could be from betrayal, broken trust, abuse, theft, physical injury, or even a fractured relationship. You must allow time to effectively mourn and process your grief to begin healing.

Dwelling on your painful emotions can cause resentments to build and complicate the grieving process. Sometimes you may even be in a state of disbelief and denial about the hurt and loss that took place.

If you are not ready to commit to forgiving, you may need to pause and ask yourself how much longer you will allow the hurt to continue having power over you and cause more distress in your life.

When you resist or withhold forgiveness, it does not harm your offender, but allows your pain to endure and build. Your healing will begin when you decide to work through the pain, hurt, and loss you suffered and commit to the forgiveness process.

The decision to forgive must come from both your mind and your heart. It is not a one-time act, but something that must be done over and over again. You cannot forgive begrudgingly or partially.

The benefits of the forgiveness process are realized when you take the time and make the effort to integrate and practice forgiveness strategies daily.

For Reflection: What are some of the challenges you have struggled with in trying to make the decision to forgive?

Affirmation: I will seek healing from my hurt and pain by committing fully to the forgiveness process with both my heart and my mind.

# 15
# A Season of Hope

*Forgiveness is the economy of the heart...*
*Forgiveness saves the expense of anger, the cost*
*of hatred, the waste of spirits.*

— *Hannah More*

In the upper Midwest, winters can be long and brutal. The cold, wind, snow, freezing temperatures, and lack of daylight keep people inside behind closed doors and curtains. Many of them get cabin fever and can't wait for the temperatures to warm up so they can start enjoying a more active lifestyle and the beautiful outdoors again.

The challenges of the winter season can have an unfortunate impact on many people's health. Some become overwhelmed by a type of depression called seasonal affective disorder, or SAD, due to the lack of sunlight. Others consume large amounts of alcohol and other substances. Many become tired, irritable, sleep longer, and notice a loss of energy.

Forgiveness is the same way. When you do not forgive, it has an adverse effect on your health. Your life becomes dark, cold, and empty of light. You have less energy and resort to unhealthy and destructive ways of coping. When you practice forgiveness, you experience renewed energy, light, and warmth in your life.

Maybe you have endured emotional darkness in your life due to an unwanted injury that occurred. As a result, you may have isolated yourself and felt sadness in your life. You may have tried to cope with the offense in an unhealthy manner. You may even have lost hope.

Without forgiveness, the cold and darkness you are feeling can last a long time and be difficult to tolerate. Forgiveness offers light at the end of the tunnel. The prospect of a season of healing, growth, and new life is just around the corner.

Those who can survive the challenges of the difficult winter months of life do so with the anticipation and knowledge that the harshness they are experiencing will soon give way to brighter days.

For Reflection: How would you describe the season of life you are in because of the suffering you have endured?

Affirmation: Forgiveness offers the possibility of hope, light, and a new direction in life as I overcome the darkness I have experienced.

# 16
# Freedom Through Forgiveness

*We win by tenderness; we conquer by forgiveness.*

— Frederick W. Robertson

$C$hoosing not to forgive has been compared to being a prisoner of your own painful emotions and thoughts. Simply put, when you do not forgive, you remain bound to the undeserved wounds and afflictions of your past. But when you do choose to forgive and no longer allow suffering to dominate your life, you are free to move on with hope.

This was the experience of a mother whose young adult daughter was killed by a drunk driver. For many months, the mother grieved and endured intense periods of hatred, anger, and bitterness toward the young man who took her daughter's life. Finally, after much difficulty, she came to the point where she could let go and forgive him.

The mother explained that she had felt like a prisoner in her own mind and no longer wanted to feel this way. Holding on to the negative emotions and thoughts about the young man who killed her daughter was destroying her life and the memory of her daughter. She was eventually able to get to a point where she could forgive this person by surrendering all her burdens and grief to God.

The strong unpleasant thoughts and sorrow that overwhelmed this hurting mother held her captive to her suffering and the grievous loss of her daughter. Only through forgiveness was she able to let go of the emotions that troubled her. That freedom gave her a new life and enabled her to live and honor her daughter's memory.

Forgiveness is not easy, but neither is being overwhelmed by distressing thoughts and feelings. Forgiving those who hurt you brings release from the past, gives you peace in the present, and allows you to move on in life with hope for a better future.

When you forgive those who have caused your hurt, you are freeing up and putting to better use the energy that once consumed your life with grudges, bitterness, and anger. Forgiveness sets you free from the desire to punish and hurt your offender.

**For Reflection:** How has not forgiving kept you captive to the painful thoughts and emotions of your past suffering?

**Affirmation:** Choosing to live a life of forgiveness frees me from being a prisoner to my wounds and the person who offended me.

# 17
# A Matter of Will

*"I can forgive, but I cannot forget," is only another way of saying, "I will not forgive." A forgiveness ought to be like a cancelled note, torn in two and burned up, so that it never can be shown against the man.*

— *Henry Ward Beecher*

Forgiving is not something most people are quick to do, especially when their lives have been significantly and terribly changed by a wrong they suffered.

After the end of World War II, Corrie ten Boom gave a speech on forgiveness in Germany near one of the concentration death camps where she was once held captive during the war. In her lecture, she spoke about how, when we confess our sins, God forgives us and our sins are gone forever.

At the conclusion of the speech, an audience member who happened to be a former guard at the concentration camp where ten Boom was once a prisoner came up to speak with her. When he met ten Boom face to face, he asked her to forgive him.

Upon hearing his request, and after saying a quick silent prayer, ten Boom reached out her hand to him and offered him her forgiveness. Though emotionally difficult for ten Boom, she understood that forgiveness was more a matter of her willingness to forgive than how she felt.

Since making the decision to live a forgiving lifestyle, there have been times in my own life when someone has done or said something that was hurtful and upsetting to me. However, in those moments, I am mindful that forgiveness is not dependent on how I may be feeling at the time. It is a choice I willingly make each time I am hurt. My forgiveness does not rely on an apology from the person who hurt me. I forgive because I know it will be better for me and the relationship I have with the other person.

For example, in different locations where I have worked over the years, sometimes people have made comments or said hurtful or insensitive words to me that are not appropriate for the workplace. They may do this because they are having a bad day or are upset about something that happened. When this occurs, I could very easily hold a grudge and hang on to my anger toward that person. Or I can choose to ignore and let go of what was said.

The same is true about forgiveness. When you make the decision to practice forgiveness strategies toward the person who hurt you, better feelings will follow.

For Reflection: What difficulties have you had between your willingness to forgive and the feelings you may have about the person who hurt you?

Affirmation: I will reflect forgiveness not only by how I think, but in my actions and how I treat those who offend me.

# 18
# Forgive from the Heart

*You have not lived today until you have done something for someone who can never repay you.*

— *John Bunyan*

Forgiveness is a choice that ultimately must come from within you. In other words, forgiveness is an internal decision you make because you want to, not because someone or something told you that you should forgive. Neither I nor this book can make you forgive another. You forgive out of the desire of your own heart.

Tracy suffered from the loss of her seventeen-year-old son who was fatally shot while walking home from a friend's house. For many years, she had no idea who murdered her son. She experienced physical, emotional, and spiritual distress. She had a stroke and became angry with God.

Many years later, after casting aside the anger and fear that had consumed her, Tracy came face to face in court with the person who took her son's life. Tracy explained how, when she met him and after all she had gone through, she was ready to offer forgiveness with all her heart. When she did, Tracy felt a great weight lifted that she had carried for many years.

In a similar way, one of the injured patrons in the 2012 Colorado theater shooting chose to have compassion for the person who killed and injured many in that horrible tragedy. The injured person explained that after he saw the shooter in court, he felt nothing but sorrow for him and offered forgiveness from his heart.

Forgiveness should not be viewed in a selfish manner or as something you do only for yourself to feel better. Forgiving another freely and voluntarily is a selfless act that takes courage and strength. It is truly a gift and an act of compassion toward your offender that must come from inside your heart without expecting anything in return. However, when you express forgiveness to the person who wronged you, mercy also comes to your life.

When you forgive from within your heart, you are mindful of the trouble you have caused others and how you have been forgiven by them and by God. You also see your offender as needing the same mercy you have received when you were extended the gift of forgiveness.

**For Reflection:** What is keeping you from forgiving freely, with no expectations or conditions?

**Affirmation:** I forgive those who hurt me, not because I should, but because I want to from my heart.

# 19
# The Strength to Forgive

*Doing an injury puts you below your enemy;*
*Revenging one makes you but even with him;*
*Forgiving it sets you above him.*

— *Benjamin Franklin*

Forgiving is difficult, no matter who may have hurt you. Any unwarranted suffering can be devastating to your well-being. Coping with and overcoming such painful offenses takes a lot of strength and perseverance.

Michele was one of three women held captive for eleven years in a Cleveland home. During that time, she was repeatedly raped and abused. She found strength during her captivity through her faith and prayer. Michele initially hated her kidnapper for the terrible acts he committed against her. Yet, through counseling and prayer, she came to see him as the sick person he was, someone in need of help and forgiveness.

A young man also found strength in a time of weakness when he was falsely arrested and accused of a crime he did not commit after the police officer fabricated his report. Because of the injustice done to him, the young man spent four years in prison before having his record cleared. Having lost everything, he was filled with anger and had thoughts of revenge against the cop who framed him. The police officer was later sent to prison for the crime he had committed against the young man.

As fate would have it, both men ended up at the same faith-based employment center after they were released from prison. They eventually became friends, and the former police officer expressed remorse to the young man he had falsely arrested. Though he had been wrongly accused and spent time in prison, the young man found strength through his faith in God and offered grace and forgiveness to the dishonest cop who had arrested him.

Finding the courage to forgive the person who unfairly hurt you can come from a variety of sources. Some victims find strength through prayer or from their faith in God. Others may find help through family and friends, therapy, or even in the forgiveness they have received from others.

You cannot change the past and the wrongs that others have done to you, but you do have a choice for how you will respond and move forward with your life. Forgiveness restores your self-esteem and frees you from emotional pain, so you can have renewed meaning in life and hope for a better future.

For Reflection: Where do you find the strength to forgive those who have hurt you?

Affirmation: I am able to forgive others because I have been forgiven.

# 20
# The Choice to Forgive

*Let us not listen to those who think we*
*ought to be angry with our enemies, and who believe*
*this to be great and manly. Nothing is so praiseworthy,*
*nothing so clearly shows a great and noble soul,*
*as clemency and readiness to forgive.*

— *Marcus Tullius Cicero*

When you have been wrongfully hurt by another, you have a choice how you will respond and cope with the offense you have experienced.

Forgiveness may not come naturally. You may initially decide to react to your ordeal through other less helpful choices. You may consider personal revenge, a legal solution, or other unhealthy coping strategies. The decision to forgive is a personal one that needs to be considered for the healing you need.

In 1986, a police officer was shot three times while on patrol in Central Park in New York City. After spending many months in the hospital, he had to learn how to live all over again as a quadriplegic. During that time, he prayed that his life would be changed so he could be released from all the unwanted, painful emotions that had built up inside him.

His prayer was answered when he made the choice to forgive the young man who shot him. The officer knew that the only way he could love his wife and child as he truly wanted was by releasing his feelings of anger, bitterness, and hatred.

Throughout history, as well as in contemporary society, the choice to forgive has been taught and encouraged. The benefits of forgiveness are emphasized in many of the sacred texts of the major religions of the world, which admonish people to practice forgiveness. Forgiveness is also encouraged in the fields of psychology, philosophy, and moral development. It can be found in many self-help books from both a secular and a religious perspective.

Choosing to forgive is a thoughtful decision that takes courage and a willingness to confront your suffering realistically and constructively. By making this choice, you are deciding to replace the suffering, which was not fair, with what is fair and beneficial and will help you to heal and find the positive outcomes you are seeking.

**For Reflection:** What are some of the benefits you would hope for in your thoughts, feelings, and actions by making the choice to forgive the person who hurt you?

**Affirmation:** I will choose to pursue the path to forgiveness, replacing the hurt I have experienced with what will bring healing and restore wholeness to my life.

# Practicing Forgiveness Strategies

*O*nce you choose the path to forgiveness and make the decision to forgive, you can begin practicing forgiveness strategies that will help you recover from the suffering you have been experiencing. As you do so, it's important to keep in mind that forgiveness is a process and a way of living that doesn't happen quickly or easily.

As you progress with your healing, remember that sometimes the path to forgiveness can be three steps forward and two steps backward. However, when you practice forgiveness daily and integrate it into your lifestyle, you will reap the benefits of forgiveness and notice peace and improved health.

It is also good to be cognizant that forgiveness is not only about your well-being. Forgiveness takes place out of a genuine concern and care for the person who hurt you as someone who has also been mistreated by others.

You do not forgive just so you will be happier, nor do you need an apology from your offender to forgive. When you choose to rise above your painful circumstances and practice forgiveness strategies, healing takes place and your life is changed.

# 21
# A Way of Living

*The brave only know how to forgive!*
*But a coward never forgave;*
*it is not in his nature.*

— Laurence Sterne

Forgiveness is a way of living or mindset, not a one-time action. There are many people who value and embrace forgiveness, but they do not know how to practice it or live it on a day-by-day basis.

At different periods in my life, I have attempted to improve my health by losing weight, eating better, and exercising. I have found that when I integrate all these activities into my daily routine and practice them on a regular basis, I experience the greatest success.

There were other times when I was not as consistent. One day I would follow my plan, but the next day I would revert to old habits. As such, I did not have as much success. The same is true about forgiveness. It is not something that you do one moment and ignore the next. It needs to become a part of your lifestyle.

A mother whose six-year-old daughter was murdered in the 2012 Sandy Hook Elementary School shooting described how a tremendous burden was lifted when she forgave the young man who killed her daughter. She learned that forgiveness is a difficult process and something you need to discipline yourself to do over and over again each time someone offends you.

To make forgiveness a part of my life, I try to remember that I have been forgiven by others and by God. This helps me to think that I am not better than those who have mistreated me and need my forgiveness. Because I have witnessed what forgiveness can do in my life, I want to share it with others.

Forgiveness is a journey. You may think that you have gone far with forgiving someone, only to have something trigger an agonizing memory or emotion. In reflection, you then realize that you might not have healed as much as you thought and need a little more work on some of the forgiveness strategies.

The path to forgiveness involves a gradual releasing of the hatred, resentment, bitterness, anger, and other painful feelings and thoughts that have controlled your life.

Keep in mind that forgiveness is not easy; it takes work and energy. It is contrary to our nature when someone injures us. But the more you practice forgiveness, the more you will benefit as it becomes a greater part of your lifestyle.

For Reflection: How can you make forgiveness more a part of your daily lifestyle?

Affirmation: I will choose not only to understand forgiveness, but to practice it daily toward those who have hurt me.

# 22
# A Change in Thinking

*He causes his sun to rise on the evil*
*and the good, and sends rain on the*
*righteous and the unrighteous.*

*— Matthew 5:45 (NIV)*

Many years ago, Rabbi Harold Kushner wrote a book titled *When Bad Things Happen to Good People*. Kushner experienced his own personal suffering and distress when his young son was diagnosed with a degenerative disease that affected the longevity of his life. In his book, he attempted to address the question of why God allows terrible things to happen to good people.

Whether they are intended or not, we all have difficult moments or tragedies in life. Such was the case for the parents of a seventeen-year-old high school girl in suburban Denver who was the unintentional victim of a fatal gunshot wound. She was shot by a classmate who was believed to be targeting an instructor at the school and ultimately turned the gun on himself.

At her memorial service, the girl's father said that he and his wife forgave their daughter's killer and asked others to do the same. He explained that the eighteen-year-old gunman didn't know what he was doing and was blinded by his own anger and rage.

While those who offended you may or may not have intended their painful actions, they are still responsible for what they did. If you look further into their mindset, you may also learn that, for one reason or another, difficult and unfortunate circumstances have occurred in their lives too.

An important component in the forgiveness process involves being able to think differently about the wrong that was done to you. Your initial reaction when you were hurt may have been to cry out and ask "Why?" or "Why me?" Tragedies or offenses may not only change your life, but they can cause you to ask heart-wrenching questions.

I am confident that I would not be doing what I am now in my life if it were not for the personal difficulties and suffering I have experienced over the years and which have changed my thinking about people and the world. Life is not always an upward, linear progression. Many times, you encounter unexpected obstacles and setbacks.

You can choose how you will think about and respond to painful situations. You can become angry and bitter, or you can consider that maybe your circumstances have opened the possibility of a new purpose in life.

For Reflection: How have your thoughts changed about your injury and the person who hurt you since it first took place?

Affirmation: I will learn and grow from the bad that others may have intended in my life, knowing that God will use it for my good.

# 23
# Reframe Your Offender

*Apologizing does not always mean that you are wrong and the other person is right. It just means that you value your relationship more than your ego.*

— Author Unknown

An important step in the forgiveness process is to reframe your thoughts about the person who hurt you. When you develop "new eyes" about what happened and broaden your understanding of the person who caused your agony, your perspective may change.

Just as there is more to who you are as a person than the injury you sustained, there is also more to the person who offended you than the wrong they did to you. They may have suffered loss, sadness, pain, and disappointment in their life, and they may be carrying a heavy burden because of some difficult situation.

The person who hurt you could be someone's son or daughter, a colleague, father, mother, relative, spouse, or neighbor. Increasing your understanding of this person and showing mercy, compassion, and empathy toward them are essential for forgiveness to occur. You need to get to the place where you see this person from more than just the viewpoint of the agony they caused you.

I work in a hospital where I frequently see many sick and hurting people. They are struggling from a variety of illnesses and injuries. As I visit with patients, I am aware that there is more to who they are than the diagnoses given for their conditions. They will often tell me about their family, work, hobbies, and other life experiences. When they do so, I begin to see each of them not just as a patient, but as a person like myself. I am then able to connect with and understand them as fellow human beings.

Expressions of compassion, along with the proper treatment and medication, contribute favorably to a patient's recovery and healing. Punishing or scolding them for what they did or did not do to contribute to their condition may hinder their compliance with treatment and their improvement.

When you show mercy to those who have hurt you, you have a more empathetic understanding of them and their life. As you express kindness and sympathy and practice compassion, forgiveness begins to emerge, and so does your healing.

For Reflection: What are some likeable attributes of your offender? What hardships in life might they have experienced?

Affirmation: There is more to who I am and who my offender is than the hurtful action that was done to me.

# 24
# Develop Empathy

*Love means loving the unlovable—*
*or it is no virtue at all.*

— G. K. Chesterton

I came from a broken home. I witnessed anger, abuse, and conflict frequently because of my father's alcoholism. When I was eight years old and my mother could no longer tolerate being mistreated, my parents divorced.

For many years, I held on to resentment and bitterness and blamed my mother for divorcing my father. I felt anger toward my father because he spent more time drinking than he did with me and my brother.

As I grew older and witnessed my father's ongoing battle and powerlessness with the disease of alcoholism, my feelings toward him changed. I learned about some of the painful experiences he had in life and saw how difficult it was for him to maintain sobriety. Sympathy gradually developed.

I also felt empathy for my mother as she endeavored to support the family by working forty hours a week in a Chicago factory. Mom was always there for me and my brother, no matter what we went through in life. She exemplified and taught us much about love, sacrifice, and character. She persevered under difficult circumstances and found strength through her faith in God.

Mom never spoke critically or poorly of my father. She supported our desire to spend time with him and make him a part of our lives. The difficulty my father had with alcoholism continued to affect not only his relationship with each of us and my paternal grandparents but also his health until he died at the age of sixty-one.

Forgiveness does not always result in reconciliation. While my mother forgave my father, they never reconciled due to his ongoing battle with alcoholism and how it affected his behavior. Forgiving my father made it possible for my mother to let go of the suffering she endured and carry on with renewed meaning and happiness in her life.

It was not until I realized how the negative thoughts and feelings I was harboring toward my parents were hurting me that I could begin to heal from my pain. When I stopped expecting my parents to be perfect and saw their lives through sympathetic eyes and empathy, my relationship with them began to change for the better.

**For Reflection:** How might having empathy and sympathy toward the person who hurt you help you to heal from the pain in your life?

**Affirmation:** My healing does not depend on changing the behavior of the person who caused my hurt, but on transforming how I think about that person and the offense I suffered.

# 25
# Be Compassionate

*The more merciful acts thou dost,*
*the more mercy thou wilt receive.*

— *William Penn*

One of the more challenging aspects of forgiveness is having compassion toward the person who hurt you, despite what they did to you. You may think that your offender is an awful person and is undeserving of any goodness or kindness from you.

In 2006, a thirty-two-year-old milk truck driver entered a one-room Amish schoolhouse in Nickel Mines, Pennsylvania, and dismissed all the boys and several women with babies, leaving eleven girls. He then fired execution style at those who remained, killing five of the girls before shooting himself. This hateful act caused significant pain and grief to many innocent people and brought much heartache and sorrow to the Amish community.

Soon after this harrowing incident, and without entertaining any thoughts of revenge, the Amish people graciously reached out with sympathy to the killer's family in both their words and their actions. In showing compassion, they were also helping themselves to heal from their painful loss.

Instead of dwelling on negative feelings and harboring hateful and revengeful thoughts toward the killer, the Amish community responded with mercy and concern toward the shooter's family. Many of them visited the gunman's widow at her home, bringing food and flowers and offering hugs to members of his family.

To some degree, you are what you think. What controls your mind affects what you do. When you express benevolence to people, especially those who have hurt you, it shows that love is stronger than hate. You are rising above the injury you suffered and bringing light into a dark situation. The despair you may feel gives way to hope, and a sense of calm comes in the midst of your chaos.

When you make the choice to practice forgiveness, thoughts of revenge and retaliation, along with feelings of anger and bitterness, are replaced by compassion, mercy, and goodwill.

The desire to wish your offender well through compassion reflects that healing and forgiveness are beginning to emerge in your life.

For Reflection: In what ways have you felt compassion for the person who hurt you?

Affirmation: Expressing benevolence and goodness to the person who injured me says more about my healing and character than it does theirs.

# 26
# Express Kindness

*Kindness is an inner desire that makes us
want to do good things even if we do not get anything
in return. It is the joy of our life to do them. When we do
good things from this inner desire, there is kindness
in everything we think, say, want, and do.*

— Emanuel Swedenborg

I love surprising people with unexpected, random acts of kindness. When my boys were young and we came up to a toll booth on the interstate, I would not only pay the attendant the money due for my car but also for the car behind us. It was always fun afterward to watch the expression of surprise on the other driver's face and see the excitement my kids had in doing a kind act.

Several years ago, I was in a car accident that was clearly my fault. I pulled out of a parking lot into oncoming traffic and was immediately hit by a pickup truck I had not seen coming due to the sun. I was personally embarrassed and felt sadness for the other driver whose vehicle was also damaged.

Fortunately, no one was injured, but I did receive a ticket for failure to yield and had to make a court appearance. When I went to the courthouse, the bailiff asked me to state how I would like to plead. I told him, "Guilty." He then directed me to appear before the judge to state my plea and told me that there would be a $150 fine, which I was ready to pay.

When I stood before the judge, I was surprised to hear him say that my ticket and fine were being dismissed. The accident would not show up on my driving record as long as I didn't have any other driving problems for the next three months. Instead of dispensing his judgment and the fine, the judge expressed kindness to me, which was a surprise I did not expect or deserve.

In a similar way, when you show kindness to the person who has hurt you, you are responding in an unexpected manner. Such grace is not only undeserved and unanticipated by your offender, but as the one expressing the generosity, it makes you feel better.

It has been said that justice is getting what you deserve, mercy is not getting what you deserve, and grace is getting what you do not deserve. Forgiveness is an expression of love that involves mercy and grace. Overcoming evil with good and showing kindness to the person who hurt you benefits both the giver and the receiver.

When you have received forgiveness in your life for a wrong you have done, why not "pay it forward" and express goodwill to those who have hurt you? Your healing depends on it.

For Reflection: Who are the people in your life who have expressed unexpected kindness to you?

Affirmation: I will show grace and kindness to those in my life who are hurting and in need of mercy.

# 27
# Wish Your Offender Well

*There is no revenge so
complete as forgiveness.*

— Josh Billings

Have you been significantly injured to the point where your
life has been permanently changed? This happened to a mother
of two when she suffered a serious brain injury and eye damage
after a shopping cart came crashing down upon her. The injured
mother felt sorry for the teenage boys who had pushed the cart
and their families, even wishing them well.

How you react and respond to the injury inflicted on you reveals
insight into your character and heart. One of the ways to know
if you are practicing forgiveness and beginning to heal can be
found in your willingness to hope for the best for the person who
wounded you. You do this by remembering that those who cause
hurt to another are also hurting. More than anything else, they
need your forgiveness and help. Wishing bad things for those
who mistreated you and hurting them even more will not help
you or them to heal.

When you have experienced an unprovoked, terrible injury, you
might say that you would not wish this to happen to anyone.
However, would you also extend the same sentiment to the
person who caused your agony?

Being able to wish for good, not bad, for the person who offended you is an important component in the forgiveness process. Expressions of benevolence and mercy are evidence that condemning judgments and thoughts of revenge have ceased.

You may have a right to negative thoughts and feelings about your wrongdoer. However, when you practice forgiveness, you choose to give up the right to damaging feelings and thoughts and to use your energy to pursue healing. By letting go of the past, you begin to see yourself and the person who hurt you from a new perspective.

The path to forgiveness is not through retaliation or payback, but through mercy and wishing the best for those who have caused your hardship. Repaying evil with evil adds to your suffering and prolongs your need of healing.

When you can desire the best for the person who injured you and practice forgiveness toward them, you will also benefit.

For Reflection: How might you sincerely wish those who hurt you the best in their life?

Affirmation: Being able to wish my offender well is a sign that healing is occuring in my life.

# 28
# Show Mercy

*Sweet mercy is nobility's true badge.*

— William Shakespeare

The pain of losing a teenage son who was unjustly killed would be life changing and excruciating for any parent. This was the case in Iran for the mother of a murdered seventeen-year-old boy. For seven years, this mother suffered and dreamed of the day when she could enact justice and take out her own revenge on her son's killer. Her grief and pain were so intense that she felt there was no way she could live with herself if she pardoned the killer and saved him from death, which in Iran was within her power to do.

The day finally came for her son's killer to be executed. The mother was faced with a difficult choice when the man stood on a chair over the gallows with a noose around his neck and hundreds of people watching. As she came face to face with the man who had taken her son's life, to the surprise of many, she slowly removed the noose from around his neck and showed mercy on him, giving him back his life.

As difficult as that decision was for her, she immediately felt a sense of relief and calm come over her. She no longer had any more thoughts of revenge. It was the expression of sympathy, not the execution of justice she had dreamed about for seven years, that brought her serenity and closure to the offense that had permanently changed her life.

No amount of revenge or anger that you inflict on the person who hurt you will help you heal. In many cases, it may make your situation and suffering even worse. By giving mercy to her son's killer, the mother finally received peace in her life and was released from the harsh emotions she had endured for many years.

Offering forgiveness to those who hurt you can often do more for you than it does for them. This mother gave a gift to her son's killer but got her life back in return. By choosing a nonviolent resolution, her actions brought light into the darkness of her life.

When you respond with mercy and charity to those who have caused your hurt, you also benefit. You cannot experience love in your heart when you have hatred in your mind. Practicing forgiveness transforms your emotional pain into peace and replaces hate with hope.

For Reflection: How have thoughts of revenge and retaliation affected your ability to express mercy to the person who hurt you?

Affirmation: I have a choice how I will respond to my loss and suffering. The decision I make will affect my life and the serenity I seek.

# 29
# Pray for Your Offender

*Our forgiving love toward men is the evidence of God's forgiving love in us. It is a necessary condition of the prayer of faith.*

— Andrew Murray

One of the last thoughts that may come to your mind when you are hurt is to pray for your offender, especially if you are consumed with anger and the desire for revenge. You may think that the person who hurt you is not worthy of your thoughtfulness and prayers.

Prayer is often associated with asking for God's help, which is something we all need in our lives. Maybe you have experienced times of weakness and despair when you have had to cry out and ask God for strength. Prayer helps you keep life in perspective when confronted with difficult or painful situations. It changes your outlook and reminds you that no one is perfect, not even you. God cares for the person who hurt you as much as He cares for you.

In 2015, when many people were killed in a Charleston, South Carolina church shooting, some of those who survived and lost loved ones did not want to give hatred a chance. Instead, they were quick to respond with prayers and forgiveness for the soul of the shooter.

In another instance, a seventy-six-year-old woman who had her car stolen by a seventeen-year-old boy and two of his friends waited seven months before she could speak to the teens in court. She explained to them that when you forgive, you not only acknowledge the wrongness of the offense, but also that there is more to the person who offended you than their hurtful action. Before giving the boys a hug in the courtroom, she told them that she prayed for them daily and that many people care about them.

Another woman who was kidnapped and brutally raped chose to forgive the man who hurt her and began praying for God to forgive him. The woman said that she asked God to help her forgive him instead of holding on to the bitterness in her heart. She explained that forgiveness set her free and helped decrease the anger and pain she suffered.

These examples show how your problems are really opportunities to practice forgiveness. Through prayer, you can find help and show compassion and mercy toward your wrongdoer.

For Reflection: How might praying for the person who hurt you help you to forgive and heal?

Affirmation: Praying for my offender teaches me humility and brings strength to my life.

# 30
# Take the High Road

*To be forgiven is such sweetness that honey is tasteless in comparison with it; but yet there is one thing sweeter still, and that is to forgive. As it is more blessed to give than to receive, so to forgive rises a stage higher in experience than to be forgiven.*

— *Charles Spurgeon*

Taking the high road when someone treats you poorly may be difficult to do because of the anger and hurt you are feeling.

Your initial thought may be to lash back in a passive-aggressive manner. This often happens during a divorce, betrayal, job termination, or similar situation. Taking the low road is usually fueled by thoughts of revenge, bitterness, and resentment.

This was the case when Marilyn found out that her husband was getting phone calls from women where he worked. She became jealous and suspicious, holding her painful emotions inside and wondering if she could ever trust him again. The couple began arguing over little things and drifting apart. Seeking to be happy again, Marilyn turned to someone else to soothe her angry feelings. It was not long before she was having an affair with a man who was also having marriage problems. She rationalized that since her husband no longer cared for her, she could do the same thing he did.

When you choose to take the low road, you may try to justify the vengeful thoughts you feel toward the person who wronged you. You may feel like a pressure cooker about to explode or a can of pop that has been shaken. In attempting to find comfort, you may even try to pull others down to your level. In times like this, it is good to pause and wait for things to calm down.

Whenever I have lashed back at those who have hurt me, it has never had a good outcome and only made things worse. My mother, who experienced her share of ill will in life, taught me that "two wrongs don't make a right."

Few people tend at first to take the high road and forgive, because it is counterintuitive to their natural instincts. Practicing forgiveness enables you to rise above your impulses to take a higher moral ground and be a peacemaker.

Choosing the path to forgiveness helps you make healthy and constructive choices. Forgiveness puts your emotions in check instead of having them lead you down a road you don't want to go. The high road increases self-esteem, maintains integrity, and helps restore harmony to your life.

Reflection: What can you do to take the high road in your life when someone unjustly hurts you?

Affirmation: I am in control of my life and reactions, and I will choose thoughts and behaviors that will help me to heal and rise above the wrong that was done to me.

# PHASE FOUR

# Experiencing the Benefits of Forgiveness

Once you acknowledge and accept the undeserved suffering you have experienced and you have committed to a forgiving lifestyle and to practicing forgiveness strategies, you will begin to see the benefits that forgiveness has on your thoughts, feelings, and behaviors.

These welcome changes might include having a new perspective on life, recognizing the tough lessons you have learned from your hurt and pain, and realizing that you are not alone in your afflictions. You may even need to seek forgiveness from others.

You may also notice that you are less negative and pessimistic and more cordial and optimistic. There is an internal freedom and peace that comes from letting go of your emotional struggle through the practice of forgiveness.

You feel better, happier, and more comfortable with yourself and the offense you sustained. You also have a genuine concern for the well-being of the person who hurt you and want the best for them.

Forgiveness restores meaning, purpose, and hope to your life.

# 31
# A New Direction in Life

*Forgiveness does not change the past,*
*but it does enlarge the future.*

— Paul Boese

Being unexpectedly and unjustly hurt can dramatically alter the direction of your life. Sometimes the offense may result in a change that affects your relationships, career, health, education, or family.

The day James heard that his older brother had been gunned down, he began struggling with a rage that lasted for many years. He felt intense anger toward the man who shot his brother. James's life became filled with hatred and bitterness. He didn't like the person he had become.

As James became aware of the effects anger was having on his life, he found help and strength through his faith in God and forgiveness. Strange as it may be, James eventually befriended his brother's killer when he was paroled from prison. Together they found a new purpose in life helping others who are at risk of legal and behavioral problems.

Though distressing feelings may be a normal reaction when you are mistreated, what you do with these sentiments is crucial for your well-being. They can get your life off course and cause you to lose direction. They can make your life spiral out of control, affect your health, destroy meaningful relationships, and create even more agony and suffering for you.

Maybe you are contending with intense emotions and a lack of ambition from the hurt in your life. You may have intense hatred toward your offender and be filled with thoughts of revenge. Others may no longer like to be around you because of the anger you are harboring. If you respond emotionally and act out in anger when you are offended, you are at risk of hurting other innocent people you care about and love.

On the other hand, your painful emotions can also be a wake-up call that motivates you to realize that what you have been doing is not working and you need to find a new way of coping and a different course in life.

Through forgiveness, you have the power to transform the energy invested in your hurt and pain into something constructive that restores and gives new meaning and ambition to your life. You can also make a difference in the lives of others. This was the case for James.

For Reflection: How might the hurt and pain you have experienced give you new meaning and direction in life?

Affirmation: Forgiving those who hurt me helps me to see what it means to have an emotionally healthy and meaningful life.

# 32
# Overcoming Hardship

*Forgiveness is a funny thing.*
*It warms the heart and cools the sting.*

— William Arthur Ward

Being unexpectedly hurt can be devastating and quickly change the course of your life. You may wonder not only why the offense happened, but what can be done to get your life back on track. Hardship is an unfortunate part of life.

After World War II broke out, an eighteen-year-old woman who had been waiting for her missionary parents to come home learned that they had been captured and killed by the enemy. She was initially consumed by bitterness, but ultimately was able to overcome her difficult circumstances with forgiveness, believing that her parents would have done the same thing.

Louis Zamperini survived a plane crash during World War II, was captured and sent to a POW camp, and consequentially suffered from post-traumatic stress disorder. Through his faith and forgiveness, he conquered the adversity he faced by never giving in to the agony he endured.

Life is filled with disappointment and hardship. But being terribly hurt does not need to define who you are or dictate your future. Adversity can sometimes bring out the best in you and give your life new meaning.

Instead of questioning why hardship has occurred in your life, it may be more helpful to think about what might be the most positive and constructive response you can make to effectively cope with it. You have a choice how you will respond to adversity. You can dwell on the awful experience you suffered or move on by exploring how forgiveness can help you overcome the hardship you've been dealt.

Forgiveness will help you heal more than retaliation. Love will help you overcome more than hate. Looking forward will enable you to get where you want to go more than focusing on the past.

To conquer hardship, you primarily need the internal strength that comes from forgiveness more than anything that external sources may provide you. Peace of mind is found when you let go of the hardship you suffered and choose how you want to think and feel about yourself.

Rather than seeing yourself as a victim, adopt the mindset that you are a survivor and conqueror, and do not let what happened keep you down.

**For Reflection:** How might making the choice to forgive help you overcome hardship and free you from the agony of being wronged in life?

**Affirmation:** My life is not defined by the hurtful actions of another but by the choices I make.

# 33
# A Gift to Others

*Until he extends the circle of his
compassion to include all living things,
man will not himself find peace.*

— *Albert Schweitzer*

Maybe you have heard the idiom "misery loves company." This phrase suggests that those who are unhappy and miserable find their situation easier to bear when others around them are also experiencing something similar.

When you are unfairly hurt, you may be tempted to tell others about your pain so that they, too, might share in your unhappiness. You may even be tempted to seek their support to justify your desire for revenge.

Some people may tell you that you have a right to be angry. They may say, "I would feel that way too" or even "I wouldn't let him get away with that." Seldom do you hear others tell you to forget about what happened, move on, overcome evil with good, or rise above it.

A twelve-year-old girl was terribly burned by ISIS terrorists and died from third-degree burns. The girl's suffering and death were especially difficult for her mother. Just prior to dying, the young girl's last words to her mother were to forgive her killers. She did not want her mother to seek revenge and become consumed with anger, hatred, and bitterness in her life. This would only cause her mother to suffer more.

When you hang on to painful feelings and continue to fuel them with thoughts of retaliation and revenge, it prolongs your ordeal and makes matters even worse.

Because of the love the young girl had for her mother, she was more concerned for her mother's healing than in punishing her offenders. The best gift you can give to those you love and care for when you have been mistreated is to encourage them to also forgive, so they will not struggle because of the wrong you suffered.

You also need to surround yourself with those who will help support you in your healing, not those who encourage negative feelings and behaviors that may pull you down even further.

No amount of punishment or revenge toward the person who hurt you will help you or others heal.

---

**For Reflection:** When you are hurting, what kind of support do you need from others to help you find strength and forgive?

**Affirmation:** I will rise above my suffering by choosing to focus on those thoughts and actions that will help restore harmony in my life and my relationships with others.

# 34
# Improved Health

*He who has not forgiven an
enemy has never yet tasted one of the
most sublime enjoyments of life.*

— Johann Kaspar Lavater

Life often becomes stressful, difficult to manage, and thrown off balance when you have been mistreated. Your health and overall well-being may be adversely affected. Depending on the offense, you may suffer emotionally, mentally, physically, socially, or morally.

These different aspects of your life are all interrelated. For example, if you have a physical injury, it may also affect you emotionally or socially. Similarly, if something happens to you morally within a relationship, it could also trouble you mentally and emotionally.

A simple way to measure how far you've come with your healing is to compare where you are now to when you were initially hurt. Are you happier and more content with yourself? What kind of thoughts are you having about yourself, what you experienced, and the person who hurt you? Have you noticed a change in your appetite, daily activity, sleep, and behavior toward the person who hurt you?

Forgiveness affects you holistically. When you begin to heal, negative emotions, such as bitterness, hatred, resentment, and anxiety, are replaced with peace of mind, lightheartedness, and optimism. Expressions of compassion and empathy gradually replace thoughts of retaliation. Forgiveness changes the downward spiral of your life and starts you moving in an upward and hope-filled direction. It restores meaning, purpose, and improved health to your life.

Studies have found that those who practice forgiveness strategies have better self-esteem, lower blood pressure, less stress, and improved sleep. Forgiveness also has been found to reduce anger, anxiety, and depression.

Forgiveness often does more for the person who forgives than the one who is forgiven. It helps you to be more successful and accomplish more of your goals in life.

Practicing forgiveness will also help increase the quality of your relationships and make you more attractive to others, because you are happier and feel better about yourself.

For Reflection: What changes have you noticed in your emotional, mental, and physical health since you began practicing forgiveness strategies?

Affirmation: I choose to let go of the suffering and pain I have been carrying and replace them with healthy and hopeful thoughts through the practice of forgiveness.

# 35
# Happiness and Peace

*If God should be as angry with me for every
provocation as I am with those about me,
what would become of me?*

— Matthew Henry

When someone hurts you, it can take away your peace of mind. It can also affect your overall well-being and the quality of your life. How you respond to those times can impact the nature of your relationships.

For many years, Steve felt resentment toward his sister and anger toward his father. As a young adult, his sister made some poor decisions that resulted in legal and financial problems. During this period, her father took money out of his estate to help his daughter, and she never repaid those funds.

The jealousy and bitterness Steve had toward his sister and father gradually fractured their close relationship. The emotional pain and negative feelings he carried alienated them from one another. Steve's preoccupation with being treated unfairly not only affected him personally, but also the relationships he had with others outside of his family.

After seeking counseling for depression, Steve realized that he had internalized his anger and resentment to the detriment of his own health. Through therapy and learning how to forgive, he was eventually able to empathize with his sister and appreciate the kindness his father had shown her.

Steve knew that if he was going to have happiness in his life again and a healthy relationship with his father and sister, he had to let go of the emotional pain that had grown over the years. He was finally able to break down the walls he had built and restore his relationship with his family.

Holding on to negative feelings toward another can have a debilitating effect on your overall well-being. It can take away your energy and satisfaction in life. Dwelling on the past and the unfair treatment you have been through also steals precious moments from your life and relationships that you can never get back.

When Steve realized that he ultimately was hurting himself, as well as his sister and father, he chose to let go of his painful negative emotions in exchange for reconciliation.

**Reflection:** What unpleasant feelings do you have from your past that you need to let go of so you can experience happiness in your life now?

**Affirmation:** I will not let the brokenness of the past determine how I feel now and prevent me from moving forward in my life.

# 36
# A Positive Outlook

*The weak can never forgive.*
*Forgiveness is the attribute of the strong.*

— *Mahatma Gandhi*

One of the favorable benefits and outcomes of forgiveness is an awareness that harmful feelings and revengeful thoughts toward one's offender have decreased. When this happens, there is also a feeling of freedom and change in perspective toward the person who hurt you.

Eva Kor's outlook on her life changed when she could forgive Josef Mengele, a Nazi doctor at the Auschwitz concentration camp who did experiments on Kor and her twin sister. Kor found emotional freedom when she decided to forgive Mengele in 1995 after realizing she could no longer live life harboring hatred.

Other Holocaust survivors have been equally resilient. Despite the horrific circumstances they faced, many have been able to exchange resentful judgments in favor of having a positive viewpoint and hope in life through forgiveness.

Studies have found that forgiving those who have offended you results in greater life satisfaction and improved mental health. You experience less stress, anger, resentment, and bitterness and greater well-being, self-acceptance, and competence to deal with life challenges. Your outlook on life changes, and you feel better about yourself and others.

Where a culture of forgiveness exists in the workplace, employees tend to be more creative, perform at a higher level, and feel more positive about their work. They enjoy coming to work and being with their colleagues.

When you hold on to negative thoughts about the person who wronged you, those thoughts are still a part of you, not your offender. Unpleasant feelings, judgments, and actions about the mistreatment you endured are not healthy and will not help improve your situation. When you choose to forgive, your attitude about what happened to you changes and so does your well-being.

Forgiveness transforms our thought patterns. It releases you from the burden and heaviness of your suffering and offers freedom and hope to your life. This, in turn, changes your perspective from pessimistic to optimistic, destructive to constructive, irrational to rational, and revengeful to caring.

Reflection: How has your attitude about life changed from practicing forgiveness?

Affirmation: As I forgive, I feel better about myself, enjoy being with others, and appreciate life more.

# 37
# Your Need for Forgiveness

*He that cannot forgive others breaks
the bridge over which he must pass himself;
for every man has need to be forgiven.*

— *Thomas Fuller*

We all have at least two things in common: first, we know what it is like to be offended by others; second, we also know what it is like to have harmed another.

When you practice forgiveness and show mercy and benevolence to those who hurt you, it is not uncommon to reflect on your own need for forgiveness too. In fact, what might trouble you more than the suffering you have experienced may be the wrongs that you have done to others.

Forgiveness is a two-sided coin. On one side is your need to offer forgiveness to those who have hurt you. On the opposite side is the reality that you need to seek forgiveness from those you have wronged.

Sometimes, you may be so offended and preoccupied with how others have offended you that you neglect to remember that you really are not that different from them. Both you and your offender are imperfect people.

Pride can hinder you from looking inward at your life and cause you to think that the person who hurt you is a worse person than you are. You might also rationalize that what they did to you is more deplorable than anything you may have done. True forgiveness happens when you are willing to take an honest and humble look at yourself.

When Jennifer Hudson's mother, brother, and nephew were murdered in 2008, she was devastated. What helped her cope was reflecting on her faith and the forgiveness she herself received from God. Hudson could have thought that she was superior to those who committed the terrible offense against her family. Instead, she was reminded that God is all about forgiveness. There was no way she could withhold forgiveness from those who took the lives of her family members.

Forgiveness might be compared to one wounded person sharing with another where to find healing. In forgiving your offender, you remember that you have also wronged others. You are mindful that if you point out the faults of others, they can also do the same to you. The reality sets in that, in the end, you and your wrongdoer are essentially moral equals and no different from each other.

For Reflection: What concerns you more, the hurt others have done to you or the pain you have caused others?

Affirmation: My willingness to forgive others is directly related to the forgiveness I need in my own life.

# 38
# Forgive Yourself

*The final form of love...*
*is forgiveness.*

— Reinhold Niebuhr

Forgiving yourself for a wrong you have done to another may sometimes be more difficult than forgiving those who have offended you.

When you are consumed with feelings of shame, guilt, and anger about an offense you committed, you may be harsher on yourself than on those who have hurt you. Though the person you hurt may forgive you for what you did, you may still find it hard to accept their forgiveness and receive the same mercy for yourself that you gave to those who hurt you.

Your difficulty with self-forgiveness may be related to your own self-esteem. You may reason that though others can be shown mercy and compassion and given another chance, you are not deserving of the same. When you withhold self-forgiveness, you continue to live with the burdens of the past. In doing so, you are also keeping other innocent people you care about and love from enjoying a happier you.

Another reason you may not forgive yourself is pride. Most major religions believe in a forgiving God. But you may reason that though God forgives you for the wrong you have done, you do not need to forgive yourself. By doing this, you are essentially saying that your standards are above those of God. You may even think that you should be held to higher standards than those imposed on other people.

Forgiving yourself can be challenging because you may have a problem seeing yourself as a flawed and imperfect human being who may sometimes do wrong and make mistakes. An essential part of growth and healing is admitting that you are a work in progress or, in other words, that you are a human being. Just as we reframe and seek to understand those who offend us from a broader perspective, it is helpful for us to do the same for ourselves. There is more to who you are than the hurt you have done to others.

When you think of and love yourself as someone who is maturing and developing, forgiving yourself becomes easier. Life offers many opportunities to change. God is also very forgiving and is not through with you yet.

Accept yourself and your imperfections. Receive the gift of mercy and grace in your life by forgiving yourself and allowing yourself the opportunity to grow and learn.

For Reflection: What parts of your life do you have a hard time forgiving?

Affirmation: Like those who have hurt me, there is more to me than the hurt I have caused. I forgive myself for the past so that I, and others, may have a better future.

# 39
# God's Forgiveness

*As far as the east is from
the west, so far has He removed our
transgressions from us.*

— *Psalm 103:12 (NIV)*

There are some people who may feel that they don't need to
ask God for forgiveness. But what if you do need forgiveness or
you recognize the wrongs you have done in your life but do not
specifically remember the person you hurt? From whom do you
seek forgiveness then?

Carrying the guilt and anxiety of the wrongdoing and suffering
you have caused others can have a horrendous effect on your
health and well-being. You may have difficulty letting go of past
wrongs you have done and be challenged with feelings of guilt,
shame, and self-condemnation. You might even wonder if God
will forgive you or what you must do to be forgiven.

Sally tells a story about how after graduating from high school,
she quickly got married, had a baby, and then divorced before
she turned twenty years old. She then began seeking comfort in
the form of drugs, alcohol, and unhealthy relationships.

Sally described herself as feeling lost and without purpose. She felt like she was fifty years old, exhausted, disgusted, and powerless to change her life. One night, with help from a friend, she prayed and asked for God's help. That prayer changed her life. Sally realized that God loved and accepted her just as she was, and value, meaning, and hope were restored to her life.

In your darkest moments, no matter what you have done or whom you have hurt, God's love, mercy, and compassion for you are greater than any offense you have committed or feelings of self-condemnation you may have. God can forgive what others will not.

There is nothing you can do to separate yourself from God's love. When you find and experience God's forgiveness in your life, you also find strength and the ability to offer it to others as well.

God's desire is to give you a new life that is free from the hurt and pain of the past. The gift of forgiveness is no more evident than in God's mercy and love for you. All you need to do is reach out and receive it.

Reflection: How does knowing God loves and forgives you affect your life?

Affirmation: God's forgiveness is greater than any wrong I have done and frees me to live my life with grace and renewed hope.

# 40
# Your Legacy

*I have always found that mercy
bears richer fruits than strict justice.*

— Abraham Lincoln

Have you ever thought about what legacy you will leave?

In December 2013, Nelson Mandela died at the age of
ninety-five. He spent twenty-seven of those years in prison
because he wanted to live his life free from the dictates of his
government. While in prison, Mandela suffered a significant
amount of cruelty for the political views he held.

After Mandela was released from prison, he chose not to retaliate
against a government that branded him a terrorist and an
outsider in his own country. Instead, he decided to forgive the
leaders of his government for their unjustifiable actions against
him. He also forgave the jailers who tried to break his body and
spirit during his long imprisonment.

When he became president of South Africa, Mandela reached
out to many of those same people in a spirit of reconciliation.
He offered some of them positions in his new government. On a
personal level, he invited a former prison guard to his inauguration
ceremony, former jailers to dinner on the twentieth anniversary of
his release, and a man who tried to have him killed to lunch.

Mandela chose to let go of the pain he endured with the hope of making a better future for all. He emphasized that it was time to put away division in his country and become united.

When you forgive, you accept and absorb into your life the hurt that was inflicted on you and let go of the desire to hurt back. You acknowledge that the cycle of pain needs to stop and, if possible, allow reconciliation to occur. For this to happen, you need to think of those who hurt you from a compassionate and empathetic perspective and have the desire to wish them well. This was Nelson Mandela's legacy.

When you forgive and show benevolence to those who have hurt you, as Mandela did, you are sending the message that mercy and kindness are more powerful than hate and evil and that the light in your life is stronger than the darkness.

In return, these actions bring healing to your wounded heart and leave a positive legacy that offers hope and bears fruit in the lives of others.

For Reflection: How might choosing the path to forgiveness, instead of retaliation, affect your legacy?

Affirmation: For my legacy, I will accept the hurt that happened, develop "new eyes" toward the person who hurt me, and work toward healing and reconciliation.

# CONCLUDING THOUGHTS ON FORGIVENESS

1. Forgiveness is rooted in God's love and forgiveness of you. Choose to let love, not hate, win in your life.

2. Forgiveness is a choice that puts you in control of your healing. Choose to respond to your hurt constructively.

3. Withholding forgiveness adversely affects your life. Rise above what was done to you.

4. Seek to understand your offender from a broader perspective with mercy and compassion and through the eyes of God, instead of through the pain you endured. You are no better than the person who hurt you.

5. Realize that you have hurt others and need their forgiveness too. Apologize for the wrongs you have done.

6. Find meaning in your pain and suffering. Choose not to live in your past hurt, but to learn from it.

7. Take responsibility and control of your negative feelings and thoughts, and choose to replace them with ones that help you to heal. You are what you think.

8. Consider how much energy you give to the wrong you suffered. Transform that energy and use it wisely for your healing.

9. Choose not to add to your hurt by holding on to painful emotions and unhealthy thoughts. Doing so hinders your healing and has a ripple effect in the lives of others.

10. Notice how when you choose to let go of your pain and suffering through forgiveness, you are blessed with a new outlook and hope in your life. Forgiveness gives new meaning and purpose.